I0560192

BLOCKCHAIN
Basics

FOR KIDS

WAGMI CONSULTING GROUP
Elizabeth Sullivan

Dear Educator,

Welcome to Blockchain Basics for Kids. A curriculum crafted with simplicity, imagination, and future readiness at its core.

As someone who grew up learning through accessible, at-home resources while being homeschooled through high school, I understand the power of clear, foundational education. That's exactly what I set out to create here: a way to introduce emerging technology concepts like blockchain in a way that is engaging, age-appropriate, and easy to teach - even if you're completely new to the topic yourself.

This program is intentionally low-tech for students - no devices or coding required - so they can focus on understanding big ideas through stories, discussion, and pen-to-paper activities. However, to make things easier for you, I've prepared all the printable worksheets, stories, and activity pages in an online folder you can access and print anytime.

Simply scan the QR code below or visit the provided link to download and print what you need, whenever you need it.

It is my hope that both you and your students walk away from this curriculum with a spark — a curiosity about the technology shaping our future, and maybe even an idea or two about how you could be part of it.

Thank you for all you do to shape young minds. If you have feedback, ideas, or simply want to connect, I'd love to hear from you. This curriculum is meant to evolve, and your insights help make it better with every classroom it enters.

With gratitude,
Elizabeth K. Sullivan
Curriculum Creator & Author
Connect on LinkedIn: @elizabethksullivan

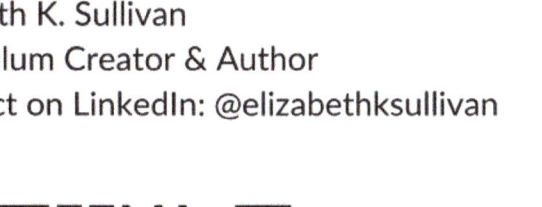

https://drive.google.com/drive/folders/1d94yoixtcblibwCuf9tlCy03HYNTCDr1?usp=sharing

WHAT IS BLOCKCHAIN

UNIT I

BLOCKCHAIN BASICS LESSON PLAN

Main discipline: Blockchain Technology Basics

Objective: Read The Blockchain Odyssey to introduce students to the basics of blockchain technology.

Other discipline: Reading Comprehension

Activity: Use the story on the worksheet to engage the class in a discussion about what problem the characters found they could solve using blockchain technology.

Other discipline: Spelling & Vocabulary

Objective: Student will increase their vocabulary with blockchain technology terminology. Worksheets include Spelling, Vocabulary, Terminology match-up

Quiz: A five question quiz for testing learned knowledge at the end of the unit

Why Teach Blockchain Technology Basics?

 Blockchain is a technology that could shape many parts of our future, from the way we use money to how we keep information safe.

By teaching students the basics of blockchain now, we are helping them understand how the digital world works and preparing them for the future. As they grow, this technology may play a big part in their everyday lives, and learning it early gives them the tools to be confident and responsible in the digital age.

Helping students grasp these concepts now will open up new opportunities for them to explore and be part of tomorrow's innovations.

1- What is a block in a blockchain?

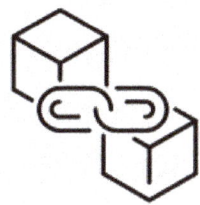

A block is a piece of data or information stored in the blockchain. It contains details about transactions, and once it's added, it becomes part of the chain of information.

2- How Does Blockchain Work?

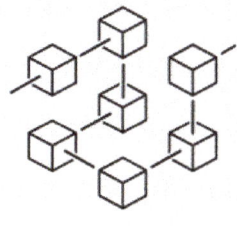

Blockchain works by storing information in blocks that are linked together in a chain. Each block is verified by many computers (nodes) before it's added, and once added, the information can't be changed without altering the entire chain, making it secure

3- Why is it hard to change information in a blockchain?

It's hard to change information in a blockchain because once a block is added to the chain, it links to other blocks. Changing one block would require changing every block connected to it, which is very difficult to do without everyone noticing.

4- What does consensus mean, and why is it important?

 Consensus means that everyone in the blockchain network agrees that the information being added is correct. It's important because it ensures that only verified and accurate information is recorded in the blockchain.

5- Why is it hard to pass off fake information once something has been verified on the blockchain?

 It's hard to pass off fake information because once something has been verified by many people (or computers) on the blockchain, everyone agrees it is correct. If someone tries to change it, the system will notice the difference, and the fake information will be rejected.

Future Applications of Blockchain Technology:

Blockchain technology has the potential to transform many industries in the future.
It could be used for digital identification, allowing people to securely verify their identity online without the need for passwords. In record keeping, blockchain can securely track and transfer ownership of important assets, such as home or vehicle titles. This would make processes like buying or selling a house more efficient. Blockchain could even be used to manage concert ticket sales, ensuring that tickets are only sold to real fans at a fair price.
Just imagine... what else could blockchain be used for?

1- Cue for You:

"Who here has ever kept a list of something important—maybe your favorite games or movies? What if everyone could see that list, but no one could change it unless everyone agreed?"
"That's kind of what blockchain does—it keeps track of important information, but no one can change it unless everyone else agrees, and that keeps it secure."

2- Story Introduction:

Read from Blockchain Odyssey where the characters first learn about blockchain technology.

Discussion Prompt:
- "In the story, what did the Scribblet discover about blockchain?
- What problems could Scribblet help to solve?"

3- Core Content: What is a Blockchain?

Blockchain is a special way to store information safely, using many different computers to make sure no one can cheat by changing the data.

Core Concepts:
- Blocks of Information: Information is stored in small parts called "blocks."
- Connected Chain: Each block is linked to the block before it, creating a chain.
- Decentralization: Instead of one person or company keeping the data, it's spread across many computers, making it harder for anyone to cheat or hack.

Teacher Cue:
- "Imagine writing down the score of a game, and instead of only one person keeping track, everyone writes down the score and agrees on it. That's how blockchain makes sure no one cheats or changes the score."

Discussion Prompt:
- "Why do you think it's important that everyone agrees on the information in the blockchain? How does that keep the information safe?"

Name_____

Expanding Sentences

Directions: Expand and complete each of the sentences

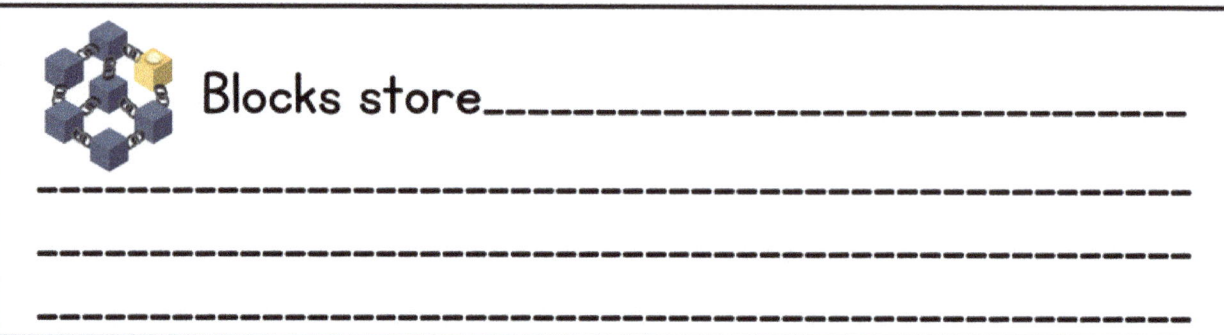

Blocks store_____

_____

_____

_____

Blockchain is secure because_____

_____

_____

_____

Consensus means that_____

_____

_____

_____

Digital recordkeeping can help_____

_____

_____

_____

Expanding Sentences

Directions: Expand and complete each of the sentences

Blocks store...

• Answer Blocks store information, like facts or data.

Blockchain is secure because...

• Answer Blockchain is secure because once something is added, it can't be changed.

Consensus means that...

• Answer Consensus means that everyone agrees before something is added to the blockchain.

Digital recordkeeping can help...

• Answer Digital recordkeeping can help by keeping information safe and easy to find.

Name _____ Date _____

SPELLING WORDS

Blockchain   Consensus   Decentralization   Security   Digital

Transaction   Innovative   Ledger   Transparency   Technology

Write a short definition for each spelling word on the lines below.

1. _____
2. _____
3. _____
4. _____
5. _____
6. _____
7. _____
8. _____
9. _____
10. _____

Write a paragraph that expresses an opinion, gives information, or tells a narrative using at least four of the spelling words.
Be sure to use complete sentences.

_____
_____
_____
_____
_____
_____

Name _____   Date _____

BLOCKCHAIN TECHNOLOGY

VOCABULARY MATCH UP

 Directions: Match the term to the definition.

TERMS

1. _____ Technology

2. _____ Consensus

3. _____ Innovative

4. _____ Blockchain

5. _____ Transaction

6. _____ Ledger

7. _____ Decentralization

8. _____ Security

9. _____ Digital

10. _____ Transparency

DEFINITIONS

A. Measures taken to protect something from harm, unauthorized access, or changes.

B. A situation where everyone involved agrees on the same decision or outcome.

C. A record-keeping tool used to track transactions or important data.

D. Tools, machines, or systems created to solve problems or improve tasks through scientific knowledge.

E. An exchange of goods, services, or information between two or more parties.

F. Creating something new or using creative ideas to solve problems in unique ways.

G. A system that securely stores and links information across multiple locations in a way that prevents unauthorized changes.

H. The quality of being open and clear, where everyone involved can see the details of actions or decisions.

I. Involving or using computer technology to store, process, or transmit information.

J. A method where control and decision-making are spread across many people or groups, rather than just one.

Name _____   Date _____

TERMS

1. __D__ Technology

2. __B__ Consensus

3. __F__ Innovative

4. __G__ Blockchain

5. __E__ Transaction

6. __C__ Ledger

7. __J__ Decentralization

8. __A__ Security

9. __I__ Digital

10. __H__ Transparency

DEFINITIONS

A. Measures taken to protect something from harm, unauthorized access, or changes.

B. A situation where everyone involved agrees on the same decision or outcome.

C. A record-keeping tool used to track transactions or important data.

D. Tools, machines, or systems created to solve problems or improve tasks through scientific knowledge.

E. An exchange of goods, services, or information between two or more parties.

F. Creating something new or using creative ideas to solve problems in unique ways.

G. A system that securely stores and links information across multiple locations in a way that prevents unauthorized changes.

H. The quality of being open and clear, where everyone involved can see the details of actions or decisions.

I. Involving or using computer technology to store, process, or transmit information.

J. A method where control and decision-making are spread across many people or groups, rather than just one.

Blockchain
Verification & Consensus

Objective

To demonstrate how blockchain verification and consensus work, showing why it's hard to alter information once verified by many participants.

Materials

- Two copies of the same heart drawing (on paper)
- A pen for your signature

Learning Outcome:

- **Verification:** Students see how information is verified by consensus, like the heart being signed and checked by everyone.

- **Consensus:** Everyone's agreement makes it difficult to introduce false or altered information.

- **Security:** The activity shows how blockchain's security comes from the fact that changes are easily spotted once the original information has been widely verified.

Blockchain
Verification & Consensus

Activity Steps

Step 1: Introduction
Explain that a blockchain stores information in blocks, and those blocks are verified by multiple participants, a process called consensus. Tell the students they will help verify a drawing (representing a block).

Step 2: The Original Signed Heart
Show the first heart drawing and sign it in front of the students, demonstrating that it's an original and verified by you. Pass the heart around the class for each student to check and sign, verifying that it's the original.

Step 3: Explain Consensus While Heart Circulates
Explain that in a blockchain, multiple "nodes" (people) must agree that the information is correct—this agreement is called consensus. Emphasize that the more signatures (verifications) the heart receives, the harder it is for someone to change or replace it without everyone knowing.

Step 4: The Unsigned Heart Trick
Once the original heart returns to you, secretly switch it with the second (unsigned) heart. Pass it around again, pretending it's the original heart, and ask the students to verify it.

Step 5: Students Catch the Fake
As the unsigned heart circulates, students will notice that it doesn't have your signature or their signatures. Ask them how they knew this wasn't the original heart, leading them to the realization that because the first heart was verified by everyone, the fake heart couldn't be accepted.

Step 6: Class Discussion on Blockchain Security

Discuss:
- How did you know the second heart was fake?
- Why is it hard to pass off fake information once something has been verified?
- What does this teach us about blockchain security?

BLOCKCHAIN
TALES

Read the story below and then answer the questions.

The Snack Tracker Solution

Ella, Max, Sophie, and Leo wanted to keep better track of who bought snacks each week. Sometimes, they forgot whose turn it was, and things got confusing.

"I think we need a better system," Max said. Ella had an idea. "Let's use something called blockchain. It's a way to keep track of information so it's always safe and organized." "What's blockchain?" Sophie asked. "Blockchain stores information in groups called blocks," Ella explained. "When a block is full, it links to the next one, forming a chain. Once we add something, like who bought snacks, we can't lose or change it." "That sounds perfect!" said Leo. "How do we add things to the blocks?" "Each time someone buys snacks, we all check the information to make sure it's correct. That's called consensus. Once we agree, we add it to the chain," Ella said. "And no one can change it afterward because it's decentralized, so we all have a copy of the chain, and everyone can see what's been added," Ella replied.

With blockchain, the group was able to keep track of their snack schedule easily. They always knew whose turn it was, and everything stayed organized.

1- Why did the friends want to use blockchain for their snack tracker?

_____

2- How does blockchain store information?

_____

3- What is consensus, and how did the friends use it?

_____

4- Why can't anyone change the information after it's added to the blockchain?

_____

5- How did blockchain help the friends with their snack tracker?

_____

BLOCKCHAIN
TALES

The Snack Tracker Solution

Ella, Max, Sophie, and Leo wanted to keep better track of who bought snacks each week. Sometimes, they forgot whose turn it was, and things got confusing.

"I think we need a better system," Max said. Ella had an idea. "Let's use something called blockchain. It's a way to keep track of information so it's always safe and organized." "What's blockchain?" Sophie asked. "Blockchain stores information in groups called blocks," Ella explained. "When a block is full, it links to the next one, forming a chain. Once we add something, like who bought snacks, we can't lose or change it." "That sounds perfect!" said Leo. "How do we add things to the blocks?" "Each time someone buys snacks, we all check the information to make sure it's correct. That's called consensus. Once we agree, we add it to the chain," Ella said. "And no one can change it afterward because it's decentralized, so we all have a copy of the chain, and everyone can see what's been added," Ella replied.

With blockchain, the group was able to keep track of their snack schedule easily. They always knew whose turn it was, and everything stayed organized.

1- Why did the friends want to use blockchain for their snack tracker?

Answer: *They wanted to use blockchain to stay organized and make sure they didn't forget whose turn it was to buy snacks.*

2- How does blockchain store information?

Answer: *Blockchain stores information in groups called blocks, which are linked together to form a chain. Once information is added, it can't be changed.*

3- What is consensus, and how did the friends use it?

Answer: *Consensus is when everyone agrees that the information is correct. The friends used it to confirm snack information before adding it to the blockchain.*

4- Why can't anyone change the information after it's added to the blockchain?

Answer: *The blockchain is decentralized, meaning everyone has a copy, so no one can change the information without everyone noticing.*

5- How did blockchain help the friends with their snack tracker?

Answer: *Blockchain helped the friends stay organized and make sure they never lost or changed the information about whose turn it was to buy snacks.*

BLOCKCHAIN IN THE FUTURE

Name _____   Date _____

Write a creative story or essay imagining how blockchain will be used in the future. Think about how this technology could change the way people interact, make decisions, and keep their information safe.
You can choose one of the following topics or come up with your own:
Future Money
Voting
Cities
Art / Music

Task: Write a short story of your idea of Blockchain in the Future:
What Will It Look Like?

Story/Essay Requirements:
- Your writing should be at least 200 words.
- Be creative! You can include characters, dialogue, and exciting scenarios.
- Make sure to explain how blockchain is being used and why it is important in your imagined future.
- Include a beginning, middle, and end to your story or essay.

_____
_____
_____
_____
_____
_____
_____
_____
_____
_____
_____
_____
_____
_____

The Blockchain

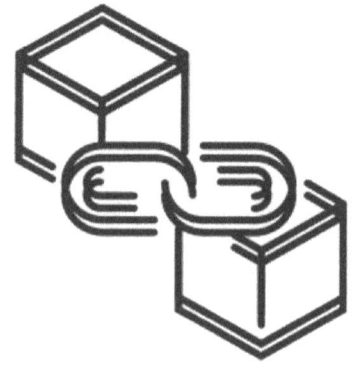

How much do you know about the Blockchain?
Answer the following questions.

1 What is a block in a blockchain?

_____

_____

2 Why is it hard to change information in a blockchain?

_____

_____

3 What does consensus mean, and why is it important?

_____

_____

4 Why is it hard to pass off fake information once something has been verified on the blockchain?

_____

_____

5 How Does Blockchain Work?

_____

_____

_____

_____

_____

The Blockchain

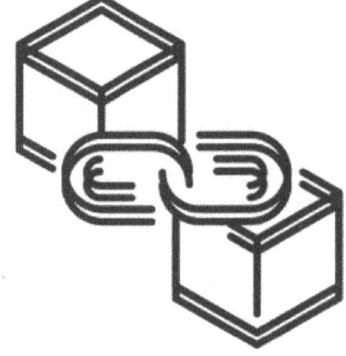

How much do you know about the Blockchain?
Answer the following questions.

1 What is a block in a blockchain?

A block is a piece of data or information stored in the blockchain. It contains details about transactions, and once it's added, it becomes part of the chain of information.

2 Why is it hard to change information in a blockchain?

It's hard to change information in a blockchain because once a block is added to the chain, it links to other blocks. Changing one block would require changing every block connected to it, which is very difficult to do without everyone noticing.

3 What does consensus mean, and why is it important?

Consensus means that everyone in the blockchain network agrees that the information being added is correct. It's important because it ensures that only verified and accurate information is recorded in the blockchain.

4 Why is it hard to pass off fake information once something has been verified on the blockchain?

It's hard to pass off fake information because once something has been verified by many people (or computers) on the blockchain, everyone agrees it is correct. If someone tries to change it, the system will notice the difference, and the fake information will be rejected.

5 How Does Blockchain Work?

For example, the thermosphere lies between the mesosphere and the exosphere. It absorbs the sun's radiation, making it very hot. This layer is home to the International Space Station and to many Earth orbit satellites.

ALL ABOUT NODES

UNIT 2

LESSON PLAN: ALL ABOUT NODES

Objective: By the end of this lesson, students will be able to:

- Define what a node is and explain its role in a blockchain.
- Understand and describe key responsibilities of nodes, including storing data, validating transactions, reaching consensus, and executing smart contracts.
- Use vocabulary words accurately and relate them to the functions of nodes

Book To Read: Welcome to Nodesville

Activity: Use the story and the worksheet to engage the class in a discussion about the roles that Nodes play in blockchain technology.

Other discipline: Spelling & Vocabulary

Objective: Student will increase their vocabulary with blockchain technology terminology. Worksheets include Spelling, Vocabulary, Terminology match-up

Quiz: A quiz of multiple choice, true - false, & short answers for testing learned knowledge at the end of the unit

Introduction to Nodes

Discussion Starter: Begin with a simple question to activate prior knowledge.

- "What is a team? Can a team work without everyone doing their part?"
- Discuss briefly and relate this to how a blockchain network needs nodes to work together.

Introduction of Nodes:

- Explain that a node is a computer or device on a blockchain network that has a specific job. All nodes work together to keep the system running smoothly and safely. Use relatable terms, like how librarians keep records or how guards protect things, and tell students they will meet nodes with similar jobs in the book.

What is one reason why nodes are important in a blockchain?

Nodes are important because they keep the blockchain network working well and make sure all the information is safe and accurate. They're like keepers of the records—if one node has a problem, other nodes still have copies of the data, so nothing is lost.

Explain what happens when nodes "reach consensus."

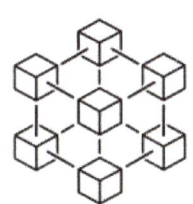

Consensus means that all the nodes agree on something before it gets added to the blockchain. Think of it like making a group decision where everyone checks to make sure the information is correct and fair. Once they all agree, it's official, and the information can be trusted.

Why do nodes need to work together on the blockchain?

Nodes need to work together to keep the blockchain secure and trustworthy. When they work as a team, they can double-check each other's information and make sure there are no mistakes or changes made without permission. This teamwork is what makes the blockchain so reliable.

Describe one job a node might have in Nodesville.

A node in Nodesville might have a job like storing data, checking trades, or protecting the rules. For example, one node might act like a librarian to store all the records, while another might work like a fairness checker to make sure every trade is done honestly.

EXPLAINING THE ROLES OF NODES IN A BLOCKCHAIN

Each node in a blockchain has a different job, and all of these roles work together to keep the network running smoothly, accurately, and securely. Here's a simple way to explain each type of node and why it's important.

Data Storage Node

- **Explanation:** "A data storage node's job is to keep a full copy of all the information on the blockchain. Think of it like a library that holds a copy of every book ever written, so no book is ever lost. These nodes make sure that if one node stops working, the information is still safe because other nodes also have a complete copy."
- **Why It Matters:** "By storing data, these nodes keep the information safe and make the blockchain reliable.

Validator Node

- **Explanation:** "Validator nodes have an important job—they check each transaction to make sure it's correct and follows the rules. Imagine you're trading a baseball card with a friend. A validator node would check that you actually have the card before the trade is made, to keep everything fair."
- **Why It Matters:** "Validation prevents mistakes and keeps the blockchain honest, so everyone can trust it."

Consensus Node

- **Explanation:** "These nodes work together to reach something called 'consensus,' which means they all have to agree on what new information is added to the blockchain. Think of it like a class vote where everyone has to agree before making a decision. This helps the blockchain stay fair and ensures that everyone has the same information."
- **Why It Matters:** "Consensus keeps the blockchain secure, so no one can add or change data without everyone agreeing first."

Security or Guard Node

- **Explanation:** "Security nodes, or guard nodes, constantly watch over the blockchain to protect it from tampering. If someone tries to change information, these nodes notice and fix the problem. They're like guards at a museum making sure no one touches the paintings!"
- **Why It Matters:** "Security nodes help keep the blockchain safe from hackers and protect all the data."

Smart Contract Executor Node

- **Explanation:** "Some nodes help run 'smart contracts,' which are like automated instructions. These contracts complete a task automatically when certain conditions are met. For example, if a smart contract says you'll get paid when a job is done, the node will make sure the payment happens as soon as it's completed. It's like having a machine that automatically dispenses your lunch once you've finished your chores!"
- **Why It Matters:** "Smart contract nodes make sure things happen just as they're supposed to, without mistakes."

Name_____

Sentence writing

Instructions: Complete each sentence below to show your understanding of what happens in "Welcome to Nodesville". Use complete sentences and add as much detail as you can!

Each node in Nodesville has an important job, such as _____

_____

_____

_____

To reach consensus in Nodesville, all the nodes must_____

_____

_____

_____

Contractor Connor uses a smart contract to_____

_____

_____

_____

Librarian Lucy records information by_____

_____

_____

_____

Sentence writing

Instructions: Complete each sentence below to show your understanding of what happens in "Welcome to Nodesville". Use complete sentences and add as much detail as you can!

Each node in Nodesville has an important job, such as storing records, checking transactions, or protecting the rulebook to keep the town safe and organized.

To reach consensus in Nodesville, all the nodes must agree on the new information before it gets added to the town's record book, ensuring accuracy and fairness.

Contractor Connor uses a smart contract to automatically complete a trade once all conditions are met, so everything happens just as planned.

Librarian Lucy records information by keeping a digital record of every transaction in the town, making sure nothing is lost or forgotten.

Name _____   Date _____

SPELLING WORDS

Blockchain   **Consensus**   **Validation**   **Secure**   **Nodes**

Transaction   **Guard**   **Data**   **Protect**   **Smart contract**

Write a short definition for each spelling word on the lines below.

1. _____

2. _____

3. _____

4. _____

5. _____

6. _____

7. _____

8. _____

9. _____

10. _____

Write a paragraph that expresses an opinion, gives information, or tells a narrative using at least four of the spelling words. Be sure to use complete sentences.

_____

_____

_____

_____

_____

SPELLING WORDS

Blockchain   **Consensus**   **Validation**   **Secure**   **Nodes**

Transaction   **Guard**   **Data**   **Protect**   **Smart contract**

Write a short definition for each spelling word on the lines below.

1. Node: A computer or device that helps run and maintain a blockchain network.

2. Blockchain: A digital ledger that records transactions or data across many computers

3. Validation: The process of checking if something is accurate or correct.

4. Consensus: When all nodes in a blockchain agree before adding new information.

5. Transaction: An exchange of information, goods, or currency.

6. Data: Information stored and shared on the blockchain.

7. Secure: To protect something from harm or danger.

8. Smart Contract: An action that automatically carries out actions when conditions are met.

9. Guard: To watch over and protect something, like a rulebook or data.

10. Protect: To keep something safe from harm, damage, or unauthorized access.

Write a paragraph that expresses an opinion, gives information, or tells a narrative using at least four of the spelling words. Be sure to use complete sentences.

Example Answer:

I think nodes are really important in a blockchain network. Each node works with others to reach consensus, which means they all agree before adding new data. This helps keep the information secure and makes sure everyone can trust it. By following validation steps, nodes check that each transaction is correct. Without nodes working together, the blockchain couldn't keep the data safe or make sure everything is fair.

ALL ABOUT NODES

VOCABULARY MATCH UP

 Directions: Match the term to the definition.

TERMS

1. _____ Transaction

2. _____ Node

3. _____ Consensus

4. _____ Data

5. _____ Guard

6. _____ Validation

7. _____ Smart Contract

8. _____ Blockchain

9. _____ Protect

10. _____ Secure

DEFINITIONS

A. A computer or device that helps run and maintain a blockchain network.

B. An exchange of information, goods, or currency.

C. Information stored and shared on the blockchain.

D. When all nodes in a blockchain agree before adding new information.

E. A set of instructions that automatically carries out actions when certain conditions are met.

F. To keep something safe from harm, damage, or unauthorized access.

G. A digital ledger that records transactions or data across many computers (or nodes).

H. To watch over and protect something, like a rulebook or data.

I. To protect something from harm or danger.

J. The process of checking if something is accurate or correct.

Name _____   Date _____

TERMS

1. __B__ Transaction

2. __A__ Node

3. __D__ Consensus

4. __C__ Data

5. __H__ Guard

6. __J__ Validation

7. __E__ Smart Contract

8. __G__ Blockchain

9. __F__ Protect

10. __I__ Secure

DEFINITIONS

A. A computer or device that helps run and maintain a blockchain network.

B. An exchange of information, goods, or currency.

C. Information stored and shared on the blockchain.

D. When all nodes in a blockchain agree before adding new information.

E. A set of instructions that automatically carries out actions when certain conditions are met.

F. To keep something safe from harm, damage, or unauthorized access.

G. A digital ledger that records transactions or data across many computers (or nodes).

H. To watch over and protect something, like a rulebook or data.

I. To protect something from harm or danger.

J. The process of checking if something is accurate or correct.

Broken Telephone
Consensus

Materials Needed

- Pre-written "message cards" with simple facts, instructions, or fun sentences (for example, "The cat wore a red hat and danced on a mat.")

- Index cards or slips of paper for recording final messages

- Space for students to sit or stand in a line or circle

Setup

Arrange the students in a line or a circle. Explain that they are each acting as a "node" in a blockchain network, and they will be passing a message (or data) from one node to the next. The goal is for the final message to match the original message as closely as possible.

Instructions

- Whisper a message to the first student in line. They then whisper it to the next person, and so on, until it reaches the last person in the chain.

- At any point, if a student thinks the message might have changed or sounds incorrect, they can ask for a Consensus Check.

- For a Consensus Check, the last three nodes in the chain compare what they've heard and try to agree on the correct message.

- Once they reach consensus, the message continues down the chain.

- When it reaches the final student, they say the message out loud and compare it with the original message.

Consensus Check Mechanism:

Emphasize that a Consensus Check can only happen if a student feels the message has changed or if they're unsure.
When they call for a Consensus Check, only the last three students (the last three "nodes") discuss what they've heard and agree on a single version of the message.
This version becomes the one that continues along the chain.

Broken Telephone
Consensus

Rules of the Game

Start with simple messages to get the students comfortable with the game, then gradually add slightly longer or funnier messages to make it more challenging.

Example messages:

- "A blue bird flew over the school."

- "The dog chased the red ball into the park."

- "Pizza with pepperoni and pineapple is my favorite."

Teacher Discussion Prompts

How Does Consensus Help?
- Explain that consensus is what keeps blockchain information accurate. If nodes didn't check the information they're passing along, it could easily become incorrect, just like in the game. Consensus helps ensure that the final data is as close to the original as possible.

Why Might Errors Happen Without Consensus?
- Talk about how errors in communication can happen naturally (like during the game). In a blockchain, reaching consensus helps prevent these "natural" errors by making sure every node has the same information.

How Is Consensus Like Working on a Group Project?
- Draw a comparison to working in groups: if everyone agrees on the same plan and checks each other's work, the end result is usually better and more accurate.

Real-World Blockchain Connection:
- Explain that just like in the game, nodes in a blockchain have to agree on data. This process keeps the data trustworthy because no single node can change information without the rest noticing.

THE BIG TRADE

Read the text below and answer the questions according to the text.

One sunny day in Nodesville, a big trade was about to happen. Ruby wanted to trade her rare baseball card with Leo, who offered her a set of collectible stickers. It was an exciting moment, and all the nodes in Nodesville jumped into action.

Librarian Lucy opened her digital record book to add the trade to the town's records, once all the other nodes agreed. Sheriff Shane checked that both Ruby and Leo actually owned what they were trading. After checking, he nodded and said, "Everything is fair—both of you have what you're trading".

Mayor Katie gathered the nodes to reach a decision, or "consensus". "All in favor?" she asked, and every node agreed. With the consensus reached, Librarian Lucy happily recorded the trade with Captain Carter and his team of Guards standing by. Then, Contractor Connor helped set up the smart contract for the trade that would release the ownership of the baseball card and stickers as soon as the trade was recorded.

Once everything was in place, the smart contract automatically completed the exchange, and Ruby and Leo were thrilled! With everyone doing their job, the big trade in Nodesville went off without a hitch, and all the nodes celebrated a successful transaction.

1- What was the item Ruby offered to trade with Leo, and what did Leo offer in return?

_____

2- How did Sheriff Shane help make sure the trade was fair and honest?

_____

3- What did Mayor Katie ask all the nodes to do before adding the trade to the record?

_____

4- What did Captain Carter and his Guards do during this transaction?

_____

5- How did the smart contract help complete the trade for Ruby and Leo?

_____

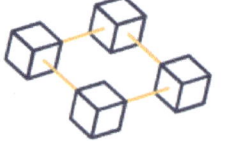

THE BIG TRADE

One sunny day in Nodesville, a big trade was about to happen. Ruby wanted to trade her rare baseball card with Leo, who offered her a set of collectible stickers. It was an exciting moment, and all the nodes in Nodesville jumped into action. Librarian Lucy opened her digital record book to add the trade to the town's records, once all the other nodes agreed. Sheriff Shane checked that both Ruby and Leo actually owned what they were trading. After checking, he nodded and said, "Everything is fair—both of you have what you're trading".

Mayor Katie gathered the nodes to reach a decision, or "consensus". "All in favor?" she asked, and every node agreed. With the consensus reached, Librarian Lucy happily recorded the trade with Captain Carter and his team of Guards standing by. Then, Contractor Connor helped set up the smart contract for the trade that would release the ownership of the baseball card and stickers as soon as the trade was recorded.

Once everything was in place, the smart contract automatically completed the exchange, and Ruby and Leo were thrilled! With everyone doing their job, the big trade in Nodesville went off without a hitch, and all the nodes celebrated a successful transaction.

What was the item Ruby offered to trade with Leo, and what did Leo offer in return?

✓ **Ruby offered her rare baseball card, and Leo offered his set of collectible stickers.**

How did Sheriff Shane help make sure the trade was fair and honest?

✓ **Sheriff Shane checked to make sure both Ruby and Leo owned the items they were trading.**

What did Mayor Katie ask all the nodes to do before adding the trade to the record?

✓ **Mayor Katie asked all the nodes to reach consensus, meaning everyone had to agree that the trade was valid. This step is important to ensure accuracy and trustworthiness.**

What did Captain Carter and his Guards do during this transaction?

✓ **Captain Carter and his Guards watched over the records to make sure no one tried to change the information.**

How did the smart contract help complete the trade for Ruby and Leo?

✓ **The smart contract automatically completed the trade of ownership as soon as the transaction was recorded**

"IF I WERE A NODE IN NODESVILLE..."

Name _____   Date _____

Welcome to Nodesville!

Imagine that you are a new node in town, and you've just been given an important job. What role would you like to have in keeping Nodesville safe and running smoothly?

Write a story or essay that explains:

- Your Job as a Node: What is your job? Are you helping store data, validating transactions, protecting the town's rules, or building things using smart contracts?
- Your Responsibilities: Describe what you do every day as a node and why your job is important to the other nodes.
- How You Work With Other Nodes: Explain how you work with other nodes to make sure everything is fair and secure in Nodesville.
- Why Your Role Matters: Why is your job important for keeping Nodesville (and the blockchain) running smoothly?

_____

_____

_____

_____

_____

_____

_____

_____

_____

_____

_____

_____

_____

_____

_____

"If I Were a Node in Nodesville..." Sample

Short Story/Essay Teachers Example Story

Example

Here's a short sample to give students an idea of what's expected.

Sample

"My Job as the Fairness Checker"

As a new node in Nodesville, my job is to be a Fairness Checker. Every day, I make sure all trades and transactions in town are fair. When two people in Nodesville want to trade apples and oranges, I check to make sure both of them actually have what they're trading. If everything looks right, I approve the trade and add it to our records.

Working with other nodes is important because we all have to agree before any trade is made. This keeps our town honest and makes sure no one is cheating or trying to trick anyone. Without Fairness Checkers like me, people wouldn't trust the system!

My job matters because without nodes like me, the whole town could fall apart. I help keep things fair and make sure everyone can trust each other. That's what makes Nodesville such a great place to live!

Reflection Questions

At the end of the worksheet, students can answer a few reflection questions to wrap up their story.

- How does your job as a node help keep the blockchain (or Nodesville) safe?

- What do you think would happen if nodes didn't work together?

- How is working as a node similar to working on a group project in class?

All About Nodes

Circle the correct answer for each question.

1 What is a node in a blockchain?
a) A type of smartphone
b) A computer or device that helps run and protect the blockchain
c) A special kind of tree
d) A place to store extra files

2 Why do nodes keep a copy of the blockchain's data?
a) So they can throw away the old copies
b) To make sure information is saved and can't be lost
c) To make it harder to find information
d) To delete data when it's full

3 What does "reaching consensus" mean?
a) Making copies of the data
b) Arguing over data
c) All nodes agreeing on new information before adding it
d) Sending data back and forth

4 Why is it important for nodes to validate transactions?
a) To keep track of how many nodes there are
b) To make sure each transaction is fair and follows the rules
c) To find out who has the most money
d) To delete extra transactions

5 What is a smart contract?
a) A paper contract that nodes sign
b) A program that automatically completes tasks when certain conditions are met
c) A contract you can only use once
d) A way to contact other nodes

Quiz: All About Nodes

Circle the correct answer for each question.

① What is a node in a blockchain?
a) A type of smartphone
b) A computer or device that helps run and protect the blockchain
c) A special kind of tree
d) A place to store extra files

② Why do nodes keep a copy of the blockchain's data?
a) So they can throw away the old copies
b) To make sure information is saved and can't be lost
c) To make it harder to find information
d) To delete data when it's full

③ What does "reaching consensus" mean?
a) Making copies of the data
b) Arguing over data
c) All nodes agreeing on new information before adding it
d) Sending data back and forth

④ Why is it important for nodes to validate transactions?
a) To keep track of how many nodes there are
b) To make sure each transaction is fair and follows the rules
c) To find out who has the most money
d) To delete extra transactions

⑤ What is a smart contract?
a) A paper contract that nodes sign
b) A program that automatically completes tasks when certain conditions are met
c) A contract you can only use once
d) A way to contact other nodes

UNDERSTANDING CRYPTOCURRENCY

UNIT 3

LESSON PLAN: CRYPTOCURRENCY

Objective:
By the end of this lesson, students will be able to:
- Define cryptocurrency and understand how it works.
- Explain why cryptocurrency is considered revolutionary and how it's changing the way we use money.
- Understand why people use cryptocurrency for purchases and what happens during a crypto transaction.

Book To Read:
Cryptonia Chronicles

Activity:
Use the story and the worksheet to engage the class in a discussion about the way cryptocurrncy works.

Other discipline:
Reading Comprehension, Spelling, & Vocabulary

Objective:
Student will increase their vocabulary with blockchain technology terminology. Worksheets include Spelling, Vocabulary, Terminology match-up

Quiz:
A quiz of multiple choice, true - false, & short answers for testing learned knowledge at the end of the unit

Introduction of Cryptocurrency

Discussion Starter: Begin with a simple question to activate prior knowledge.

What is Cryptocurrency?

Cryptocurrency is a type of money that exists only online. Unlike cash or coins, it's digital and doesn't rely on banks or governments to work. Instead, it's managed through a system called blockchain, which keeps it safe and secure. You can send or receive cryptocurrency using a phone, computer, or tablet.

Why is Cryptocurrency Special?

Cryptocurrency is changing how people use money by making it faster, safer, and easier to access. Since it's decentralized, no single person, company, or government controls it. Transactions can happen instantly, anywhere in the world. Blockchain technology also ensures that all transactions are secure and protected from tampering, making it a reliable way to use money online.

How is Cryptocurrency Different From Regular Money?

Cryptocurrency doesn't need a middleman like a bank to process payments. Instead, you can send it directly to someone else, no matter where they are in the world. This makes it much faster and often cheaper than using traditional money or credit cards.

Why Do People Use Cryptocurrency?

People use cryptocurrency because it's fast, secure, and easy to use. Transactions happen quickly, and are protected from fraud or tampering, making it a safe option for digital payments. Even if the sender and receiver are in different countries. Anyone with a digital wallet and internet access can use it, making it helpful for people who might not have a bank account.

What Happens When You Use Cryptocurrency?

"When you use cryptocurrency to make a purchase, the process is simple. First, you send the cryptocurrency from your digital wallet to the seller's wallet. The blockchain then records the transaction, and the system checks that everything is correct. Once verified, the payment is complete and cannot be changed or altered.

Why is Blockchain Important?

Blockchain is what makes cryptocurrency possible. It keeps transactions secure by ensuring that no one can change them once they're recorded. If someone wanted to make a correction then a new block of information would need to be created. The blockchain is also transparent, meaning everyone involved can see the records. And it is more reliable because it's managed by many computers working together instead of one person or company.

EXPLAINING HOW IS CRYPTOCURRENCY CREATED?

How is Traditional Money Created?

Traditional money, like dollars or coins, is created by governments and printed in factories called mints. Banks then distribute this money to people through ATMs and other systems. Governments control how much money is printed, and they decide when to make more or less depending on the economy.

How is Cryptocurrency Created?

Cryptocurrency isn't printed like traditional money. Instead, it is created digitally through processes called mining and minting. These methods use computers and technology to add new cryptocurrency to the blockchain.

What is Mining?

Mining is like solving a super hard puzzle on a computer. Special computers called miners work to solve these puzzles, and when they do, they are rewarded with new cryptocurrency. Each solved puzzle adds a new block to the chain.

- Example: Imagine you're racing to solve a math problem. The first person to solve it gets a prize. That's how mining works, but with very complicated math problems!

What is Minting?

Minting is another way cryptocurrency is created. Instead of solving puzzles, minting happens automatically when people lock their existing cryptocurrency in the system to help it work better. This process is often used with Proof of Stake, where participants "stake" their cryptocurrency and, in return, earn new coins.
- Example: Imagine you plant seeds (your cryptocurrency) in a garden (the blockchain), and after a while, new fruits (new cryptocurrency) grow. That's how minting works!

How is This Different from Printing Money?

Traditional money is created by governments who decide how much to print and when to print it. This process requires special factories, machines, and lots of decisions about how money should flow through the economy.

Cryptocurrency, on the other hand, is created digitally through mining and minting. No single person, company, or government decides how much to make. Instead, the rules for creating cryptocurrency are built into the blockchain system, which ensures that new cryptocurrency is created fairly, securely, and automatically.

This makes it different from traditional money because it isn't controlled by any one group—it's managed by the people who use it.

Why is This Important?

Cryptocurrency is created using rules called protocols. These protocols are like a set of instructions that everyone has to follow, keeping the system fair and secure. For example, think about a board game where the rules ensure no one can cheat—it keeps the game fun and fair for everyone.

What makes cryptocurrency special is that it allows people not just to use money but also to help create and own it. This is important for people who may not have access to traditional banks or money systems. By following these fair rules, anyone with a computer or internet can participate in the system, send and receive money, and even be part of creating new cryptocurrency. It's a way for more people to take part in how money works, no matter where they live.

Name_____

Sentence writing

Instructions: Finish each sentence below with your own ideas. Use complete sentences and add as much detail as you can!

Cryptocurrency is important in Cryptonia because _____

_____

_____

_____

If I had a digital wallet, I would use it to _____

_____

_____

_____

The blockchain keeps transactions safe by _____

_____

_____

_____

One thing I learned about cryptocurrency is _____

_____

_____

_____

Answer Key

Sentence writing

Instructions: Finish each sentence below with your own ideas. Use complete sentences and add as much detail as you can!

Cryptocurrency is important in Cryptonia because it allows people to buy and sell things without using cash or banks.

If I had a digital wallet, I would use it to buy items online and send money to my friends.

The blockchain keeps transactions safe by recording everything so no one can change it or cheat.

One thing I learned about cryptocurrency is that it is digital money that can be used all over the world.

Name _____ Date _____

SPELLING WORDS

Efficiency	Adoption	Verification	Ledger	Ownership
Transparency	Virtual	Automation	Fairness	Judge

Write a short definition for each spelling word on the lines below.

1. _____

2. _____

3. _____

4. _____

5. _____

6. _____

7. _____

8. _____

9. _____

10. _____

Write a paragraph that expresses an opinion, gives information, or tells a narrative using at least four of the spelling words. Be sure to use complete sentences.

_____

_____

_____

_____

_____

_____

SPELLING WORDS

Efficiency	**Adoption**	**Verification**	**Ledger**	**Ownership**
Transparency	**Virtual**	**Automation**	**Fairness**	**Judge**

Write a short definition for each spelling word on the lines below.

1. Efficiency: The ability to do something well without wasting time or resources.

2. Adoption: The act of legally taking something or someone as your own

3. Verification: The process of checking that something is correct, true, or genuine

4. Ledger: A book or system for keeping records of transactions or agreements.

5. Ownership: The legal right or control over something, like owning a pet or an item.

6. Transparency: Where actions and decisions are visible to everyone involved.

7. Virtual: Existing in digital or online form, rather than in the physical world.

8. Automation: The process of using machines or technology to do tasks without humans.

9. Fairness: The quality of making judgments that are free from bias or favoritism.

10. Judge: A person who evaluates or makes decisions in competitions.

Write a paragraph that expresses an opinion, gives information, or tells a narrative using at least four of the spelling words. Be sure to use complete sentences.

Example Answer:

I think smart contracts are really cool because they make sure everything is done with fairness and no one can cheat. Since they are on the blockchain, they follow automation and complete tasks automatically. If I bought a game item, the transaction would go through as soon as I pay. I like that smart contracts make things fast and fair!

CRYPTOCURRENCY

VOCABULARY MATCH UP

 Directions: Match the term to the definition.

TERMS

1. _____ Cryptocurrency

2. _____ Blockchain

3. _____ Wallet

4. _____ Decentralized

5. _____ Transaction

6. _____ Mining

7. _____ Seed Phrase

8. _____ Secure

9. _____ Accessible

10. _____ Exchange

DEFINITIONS

A. A digital form of money that exists only online.

B. A series of blocks where digital information is stored securely.

C. A set of words used to recover access to a digital wallet.

D. A digital tool used to store and send cryptocurrency.

E. The exchange of goods, services, or money between people.

F. The act of creating new cryptocurrency by solving complex problems.

G. Not controlled by a single person, group, or bank.

H. To watch over and protect something, like a rulebook or data.

I. Protected from theft or tampering.

J. A platform or process where cryptocurrency is bought, sold, or traded.

Name _____   Date _____

CRYPTOCURRENCY
VOCABULARY MATCH UP
ANSWER KEY

TERMS

1. __A__ Cryptocurrency

2. __B__ Blockchain

3. __D__ Wallet

4. __G__ Decentralized

5. __E__ Transaction

6. __F__ Mining

7. __C__ Seed Phrase

8. __I__ Secure

9. __H__ Accessible

10. __J__ Exchange

DEFINITIONS

A. A digital form of money that exists only online.

B. A series of blocks where digital information is stored securely.

C. A set of words used to recover access to a digital wallet.

D. A digital tool used to store and send cryptocurrency.

E. The exchange of goods, services, or money between people.

F. The act of creating new cryptocurrency by solving complex problems.

G. Not controlled by a single person, group, or bank.

H. To watch over and protect something, like a rulebook or data.

I. Protected from theft or tampering.

J. A platform or process where cryptocurrency is bought, sold, or traded.

Design your own
Cryptocurrency Coin

ⓘ Instructions

Name of your coin: _____

Purpose of your coin: _____

_____

_____

Draw and color your coin below. Include symbols, colors, or designs that represent its purpose.

Design your own Cryptocurrency Coin

Teacher Discussion Prompts

Before the Activity:
- "Why do you think different cryptocurrency coins have different purposes? What are some examples of things cryptocurrency could be used for in our world?"
- "If you were to invent a coin, what problem would it solve, or how would it help people?"

During the Activity:
- "What does your coin's design say about its purpose? Are there any symbols, colors, or shapes that help explain what your coin is for?"
- **"**How will people use your coin? Is it for something online, like gaming, or for real-world uses, like buying food or helping the planet?"

After Presentations:
- **"**Which coin do you think would be the most helpful in our community, and why?"
- **"**What makes a cryptocurrency coin successful? Do you think it's the way it looks, what it's used for, or something else?"
- **"**What's one thing you learned about designing cryptocurrency coins from this activity?"

Extension Discussion Ideas

Real-World Connection:
- "If you could combine ideas from two coins we've learned about, like Bitcoin and Cardano, what new coin would you make? What could it do?"

Ethical Considerations:
- "What responsibilities do we have when creating a new type of money? How can we make sure it's fair and helps everyone?"

Design your own
Cryptocurrency
Coin

Objective:

Teach students how cryptocurrencies represent digital value, provide real-world solutions, and encourage creativity.

Activity Instructions

Introduction:
Discuss how cryptocurrencies like Bitcoin and Ethereum are digital currencies with unique purposes.

Activity:
Each student designs their own cryptocurrency coin.
They name their coin, decide its purpose (e.g., buying games, helping the environment), and add creative designs to represent its value or goal.
Optional: Students can write a short description of their coin explaining why someone would want to use it.

Showcase:
Students present their coin to the class, explaining its features, what it does, and what makes it special.

Classmates can "vote" for the most creative or useful coin.

Summary Statement:

"Today, we explored how cryptocurrencies can have different purposes and solve unique problems, just like the coins you created. Your designs show how creative and practical cryptocurrency can be, whether it's for helping others, buying digital items, or improving the world around us. By understanding how these coins work and imagining new ones, you've taken a big step toward thinking like innovators and problem-solvers in a digital world. Great job, everyone!"

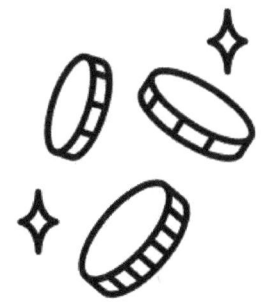

Design your own
Cryptocurrency
Coin

(i) **Instructions**

Name of your coin: _____

Purpose of your coin: _____

_____

_____

Draw and color your coin below. Include symbols, colors, or designs that represent its purpose.

NO POCKETS, NO PROBLEM!

Read the story below and then answer the questions.

In Cryptonia, no one carried coins—they used cryptocurrency! Lila loved her digital wallet because it made buying things so easy. She didn't have to worry about losing her money or finding a place to carry it. All she needed was her phone.

One sunny afternoon, Lila walked to the marketplace and spotted the most amazing shiny hoverboard. Its metallic paint sparkled under the sunlight, and it had neon wheels that glowed with every turn. "I have to have it!" she thought, imagining herself zipping through Cryptonia in style.

Lila opened her wallet app, scanned the seller's QR code, and tapped "Send." Instantly, the blockchain recorded her payment, and the hoverboard was hers. The seller grinned and said, "Enjoy the ride!" Lila hopped on, feeling the smooth glide as the hoverboard picked up speed. No cash, no waiting, no problems.

As she zoomed through Cryptonia, weaving around friends and waving to shopkeepers, she shouted, "Who needs pockets when you've got crypto?" Then she laughed and added, "Oh no—now where do I put my phone?"

1- What did Lila use instead of coins in Cryptonia?

_____

2- What did Lila want to buy at the marketplace?

_____

3- How did Lila pay for her hoverboard?

_____

4- What did the blockchain do after Lila made her payment?

_____

5- Why did Lila think cryptocurrency was the best?

_____

NO POCKETS, NO PROBLEM!

In Cryptonia, no one carried coins—they used cryptocurrency! Lila loved her digital wallet because it made buying things so easy. She didn't have to worry about losing her money or finding a place to carry it. All she needed was her phone.

One sunny afternoon, Lila walked to the marketplace and spotted the most amazing shiny hoverboard. Its metallic paint sparkled under the sunlight, and it had neon wheels that glowed with every turn. "I have to have it!" she thought, imagining herself zipping through Cryptonia in style.

Lila opened her wallet app, scanned the seller's QR code, and tapped "Send." Instantly, the blockchain recorded her payment, and the hoverboard was hers. The seller grinned and said, "Enjoy the ride!" Lila hopped on, feeling the smooth glide as the hoverboard picked up speed. No cash, no waiting, no problems.

As she zoomed through Cryptonia, weaving around friends and waving to shopkeepers, she shouted, "Who needs pockets when you've got crypto?" Then she laughed and added, "Oh no—now where do I put my phone?

✅ What did Lila use instead of coins in Cryptonia?
Lila used cryptocurrency instead of coins

✅ What did Lila want to buy at the marketplace?
Lila wanted to buy a shiny hoverboard.

✅ How did Lila pay for her hoverboard?
Lila paid by scanning the seller's QR code with her wallet app.

✅ What did the blockchain do after Lila made her payment?
The blockchain recorded her payment, making sure it was secure.

✅ Why did Lila think cryptocurrency was the best?
Lila thought cryptocurrency was the best because she didn't need pockets or cash.

"A DAY IN CRYPTONIA..."

Name _____ Date _____

A Day in Cryptonia

Imagine you live in Cryptonia, a digital city where everything runs on cryptocurrency instead of regular money.

Write a short essay describing your experience in Cryptonia. Use your imagination!

1. What is a normal day like in Cryptonia?
How do people buy things without using cash or credit cards?
What kinds of things can you buy with cryptocurrency?
2. How do people keep their money safe in Cryptonia?
Where do they store their cryptocurrency?
What happens if someone loses their digital wallet?
3. What makes Cryptonia different from the world we live in today?
Is it easier, safer, or more fun?
Would you want to live there forever? Why or why not?

_____
_____
_____
_____
_____
_____
_____
_____
_____
_____
_____

"A Day in Cryptonia..."

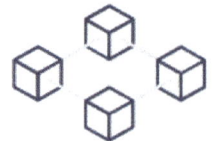

Short Story/Essay Teachers Guide

Objective

Students will explore the concept of cryptocurrency and digital transactions by imagining a world where all money is digital.

Instructions

Write a story or essay that explains:

1. What is a normal day like in Cryptonia?
How do people buy things without using cash or credit cards?
What kinds of things can you buy with cryptocurrency?
2. How do people keep their money safe in Cryptonia?
Where do they store their cryptocurrency?
What happens if someone loses their digital wallet?
3. What makes Cryptonia different from the world we live in today?
Is it easier, safer, or more fun?
Would you want to live there forever? Why or why not?

Story Prompts

(These prompts can help students get started.)

- "Every day, I use cryptocurrency to..."
- "Cryptonia is different from my world because..."
- "I keep my digital wallet safe by..."
- "One thing I like about living in Cryptonia is..."

Requirements

- 1-3 paragraphs describing life in Cryptonia.
- Use at least two cryptocurrency-related terms (e.g., blockchain, digital wallet, transaction).
- Be creative and descriptive – make Cryptonia feel real!
- Answer at least one story prompt in detail.

"A Day in Cryptonia..."

Short Story/Essay Teachers Example Story

Example

Here's a short sample to give students an idea of what's expected.

Sample

"Life in Cryptonia is pretty different from what I'm used to, but I think I like it! This morning, I went to my favorite smoothie shop and paid for my drink using my digital wallet—no cash or card, just a quick scan, and boom, transaction complete!

Later, my friend and I traded some cool digital sneakers online. Since everything is recorded on the blockchain, we didn't have to worry about scams or someone taking our stuff without paying. It's like having a receipt that never gets lost!

The only tricky part? My grandpa came to visit, and he had no idea how to use cryptocurrency. He kept asking, 'Where's the cash? How do I hold it?' It made me realize that not everyone is used to this new way of paying.

I think Cryptonia is really fun because everything is fast and secure, but I'd still want to keep some real cash, just in case!"

Reflection Questions

At the end of the worksheet, students can answer a few reflection questions to wrap up their story.

- How is money in Cryptonia different from the money we use today?

- What are some possible challenges or risks of a world without physical money?

- Would you want to live in Cryptonia? Why or why not?

- What new inventions or technology would make Cryptonia even better?

Cryptocurrency

Circle the correct answer for each question.

1 What is cryptocurrency?
A. Paper money you can touch
B. A digital form of money that exists only online and is secured by blockchain technology
C. A special coin you keep in your pocket
D. A type of bank account

2 How does the blockchain keep cryptocurrency secure?
A. It erases all records of transactions
B. It hides transactions so no one can see them
C. It records all transactions in a tamper-proof ledger
D. It lets people make changes whenever they want

3 What does it mean when cryptocurrency is decentralized?
A. It's controlled by a government or bank
B. It's not controlled by one person, group, or bank
C. It's kept in one central place for everyone to use
D. It requires everyone to meet in person to trade

4 What is a digital wallet used for?
A. To store and send cryptocurrency
B. To print cryptocurrency on paper
C. To lock your computer
D. To keep track of your cash and coins

5 Why might someone prefer cryptocurrency over traditional money?
A. It's slower and harder to use
B. It's faster, more secure, and doesn't require banks or intermediaries
C. It works only in some countries
D. It can only be used with coins and paper money

Quiz: Cryptocurrency

Circle the correct answer for each question.

What is cryptocurrency?

1 A. Paper money you can touch

B. A digital form of money that exists only online and is secured by blockchain technology

C. A special coin you keep in your pocket

D. A type of bank account

2 How does the blockchain keep cryptocurrency secure?

A. It erases all records of transactions

B. It hides transactions so no one can see them

C. It records all transactions in a tamper-proof ledger

D. It lets people make changes whenever they want

3 What does it mean when cryptocurrency is decentralized?

A. It's controlled by a government or bank

B. It's not controlled by one person, group, or bank

C. It's kept in one central place for everyone to use

D. It requires everyone to meet in person to trade

4 What is a digital wallet used for?

A. To store and send cryptocurrency

B. To print cryptocurrency on paper

C. To lock your computer

D. To keep track of your cash and coins

5 Why might someone prefer cryptocurrency over traditional money?

A. It's slower and harder to use

B. It's faster, more secure, and doesn't require banks or intermediaries

C. It works only in some countries

D. It can only be used with coins and paper money

SMART CONTRACTS MADE SIMPLE

UNIT 4

LESSON PLAN: SMART CONTRACTS

Objective:
By the end of this lesson, students will be able to:

- Define smart contracts and explain how they work.
- Understand how smart contracts automate transactions through "if-then" logic.
- Identify real-world examples of smart contracts in gaming, finance, and other industries.
- Discuss the benefits of smart contracts, including security, transparency, and reliability.
- Reflect on the emotional and ethical aspects of smart contracts in everyday life.

Book To Read:
Pixel Perfect Pets

Activity:
Use the story and the worksheet to engage the class in a discussion about how smart contracts can be used in blockchain technology.

Other discipline:
Spelling & Vocabulary

Objective:
Student will increase their vocabulary with blockchain technology terminology. Worksheets include Spelling, Vocabulary, Terminology match-up

Quiz:
A quiz of multiple choice, true - false, & short answers for testing learned knowledge at the end of the unit

Introduction to Smart Contracts

Discussion Starter: Begin with a simple question to activate prior knowledge.

- "Has anyone ever made a pinky promise? What happens if you break that promise?"
- "A smart contract is like a pinky promise that can't be broken because it's run by code on the internet. It makes sure both sides keep their promises."
- "Let's think about how Paige adopts Pixel using a smart contract. What steps happen automatically once she makes the decision?"

What is a smart contract?

 A smart contract is a digital agreement stored on the blockchain that runs automatically when certain conditions are met. It follows an "if-then" rule, meaning it only completes an action when the requirements are fulfilled—without needing a person to check.

How do smart contracts work?

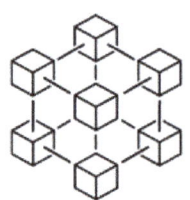 Smart contracts are made up of code that tells them exactly what to do. When two people agree on something, the smart contract records the agreement on the blockchain and executes the deal automatically when both sides meet their conditions.

Why do people use smart contracts instead of regular agreements?

 Smart contracts remove the need for middlemen like banks, lawyers, or companies. They make transactions faster, safer, and fairer because everything is recorded and can't be changed once it's on the blockchain.

How do smart contracts help make things fair?

 Smart contracts follow set rules and can't be changed, so no one can cheat or back out of a deal once it's made. Everything is recorded on the blockchain, making it transparent and secure.

What happens if someone tries to change a smart contract after it's created?

Once a smart contract is placed on the blockchain, it can't be changed. This is called immutability—it means no one can edit or erase the agreement, making it secure and trustworthy.

What are some real-life examples of smart contracts?

Smart contracts are used for many things, including:

- Online gaming (automatic trading of items)
- Buying and selling digital art (NFTs)
- Paying for event tickets (stopping fake ticket sales)
- Smart home systems (unlocking doors only for approved people)

Why are smart contracts important for the future?

Smart contracts make transactions faster, safer, and fairer. Some businesses are starting to use them to help people trade, buy, and sell things automatically without needing a bank or company to approve every step.

Wrap-Up Discussion Prompts:

- Would you trust a smart contract to handle an important agreement for you? Why or why not?

- Can you think of something in your life that could be improved with a smart contract?

- If you could create a smart contract, what would it do?

Name_____

Sentence writing

Instructions: Finish each sentence below with your own ideas.
Use complete sentences and add as much detail as you can!

One reason smart contracts are helpful is that they _____

If I wanted to trade a game with a friend, a smart contract could

----

A smart contract could help me remember to _____

One thing I learned about smart contracts is _____

Sentence writing

Instructions: Finish each sentence below with your own ideas. Use complete sentences and add as much detail as you can!

One reason smart contracts are helpful is that they make sure both sides of an agreement follow the rules without needing a person to check.

If I wanted to trade a video game with a friend, a smart contract could make sure we both send our games at the same time so no one backs out of the trade.

If I could use a smart contract in my own life, I would use it to automatically save my allowance every week so I don't forget.

One thing I learned about smart contracts is that once they are on the blockchain, no one can change them, so they are very secure.

Name _____ Date _____

SPELLING WORDS

Efficiency	Adoption	Verification	Ledger	Ownership
Transparency	Virtual	Automation	Fairness	Judge

Write a short definition for each spelling word on the lines below.

1. _____

2. _____

3. _____

4. _____

5. _____

6. _____

7. _____

8. _____

9. _____

10. _____

Write a paragraph that expresses an opinion, gives information, or tells a narrative using at least four of the spelling words. Be sure to use complete sentences.

_____

_____

_____

_____

_____

_____

SPELLING WORDS

Efficiency	**Adoption**	**Verification**	**Ledger**	**Ownership**
Transparency	**Virtual**	**Automation**	**Fairness**	**Judge**

Write a short definition for each spelling word on the lines below.

1. Efficiency: The ability to do something well without wasting time or resources.

2. Adoption: The act of legally taking something or someone as your own

3. Verification: The process of checking that something is correct, true, or genuine

4. Ledger: A book or system for keeping records of transactions or agreements.

5. Ownership: The legal right or control over something, like owning a pet or an item.

6. Transparency: Where actions and decisions are visible to everyone involved.

7. Virtual: Existing in digital or online form, rather than in the physical world.

8. Automation: The process of using machines or technology to do tasks without humans.

9. Fairness: The quality of making judgments that are free from bias or favoritism.

10. Judge: A person who evaluates or makes decisions in competitions.

Write a paragraph that expresses an opinion, gives information, or tells a narrative using at least four of the spelling words. Be sure to use complete sentences.

Example Answer:

I think smart contracts are really cool because they make sure everything is done with fairness and no one can cheat. Since they are on the blockchain, they follow automation and complete tasks automatically. If I bought a game item, the transaction would go through as soon as I pay. I like that smart contracts make things fast and fair!

SMART CONTRACTS

VOCABULARY MATCH UP

 Directions: Match the term to the definition.

TERMS

1. _____ Adoption

2. _____ Automation

3. _____ Ownership

4. _____ Transparency

5. _____ Judge

6. _____ Ledger

7. _____ Virtual

8. _____ Fairness

9. _____ Verification

10. _____ Efficiency

DEFINITIONS

A. The process of checking that something is correct, true, or genuine.

B. The quality of making judgments that are free from bias or favoritism.

C. The act of legally taking something or someone as your own, such as adopting a pet.

D. A book or system for keeping records of transactions or agreements.

E. A person who evaluates or makes decisions in competitions.

F. The process of using machines or technology to perform tasks without human involvement.

G. The legal right or control over something, like owning a pet or an item.

H. Existing in digital or online form, rather than in the physical world.

I. Openness and clarity, where actions and decisions are visible to everyone involved.

J. The ability to do something well without wasting time or resources.

SMART CONTRACTS
VOCABULARY MATCH UP
ANSWER KEY

TERMS

1. __C__ Adoption

2. __F__ Automation

3. __G__ Ownership

4. __I__ Transparency

5. __E__ Judge

6. __D__ Ledger

7. __H__ Virtual

8. __B__ Fairness

9. __A__ Verification

10. __J__ Efficiency

DEFINITIONS

A. The process of checking that something is correct, true, or genuine.

B. The quality of making judgments that are free from bias or favoritism.

C. The act of legally taking something or someone as your own, such as adopting a pet.

D. A book or system for keeping records of transactions or agreements.

E. A person who evaluates or makes decisions in competitions.

F. The process of using machines or technology to perform tasks without human involvement.

G. The legal right or control over something, like owning a pet or an item.

H. Existing in digital or online form, rather than in the physical world.

I. Openness and clarity, where actions and decisions are visible to everyone involved.

J. The ability to do something well without wasting time or resources.

Blockchain Voting Simulation

Rules of the Game

1. One vote, one student:
Each student gets only one vote.

2. Consensus before counting: Every ballot must be verified by the class (or a select group) before it is added to the blockchain.

3. Immutable votes: Once a vote is verified and added to the
 blockchain, it cannot be changed.

Teacher Discussion Prompts

Why did we need to verify the votes before adding them to the blockchain?

What would happen if someone tried to change their vote after it was added to the blockchain?

How does this voting game show the fairness and security of blockchain technology?

Setup

Decide on a class decision that the students will vote on (e.g., what type of movie to watch, which snack to bring). - Prepare ballots (index cards) with space for students to cast their vote.

Blockchain Voting
Simulation

Materials Needed

- Index cards or small slips of paper for ballots

- A chalkboard, whiteboard, or large sheet of paper for tallying votes - Markers or pens

- String or tape to create the 'blockchain' of votes

Instructions

Step 1: Voting - Present the class with a question to vote on, such as: - 'What snack should we have on Friday?' (e.g., popcorn, cookies, fruit) - 'What type of movie should we watch?' (e.g., comedy, action, animation) - Each student writes their vote on an index card (ballot), without showing anyone.

Step 2: Verification and Consensus - Collect the ballots and ask students to serve as 'verifiers.' Each vote must be verified by several students (acting as nodes) to ensure it is correct. They check that the vote is valid (i.e., one vote per student, no invalid choices). - Once the vote is verified, it is recorded on the blockchain (by linking the ballots with string or tape, creating a chain of votes).

Step 3: Securing the Blockchain - After all votes are verified, add each ballot to the chain. The order of votes must stay the same, and no changes can be made after they are added. - The verified votes are now linked together, and the voting results cannot be tampered with.

Step 4: Tallying Votes - The teacher tallies the votes by referring to the blockchain of verified ballots. The result is now final, and no changes can be made to the blockchain.

THE SMART CONTRACT SURPRISE

Read the story below and then answer the questions.

In Bitville, people used smart contracts to make sure deals were fair. If you wanted to buy something, enter a contest, or even rent a bike, a smart contract handled everything automatically!

Milo had been saving up to buy a virtual pet—a Pixel Pals cat. The best part? The adoption process used a smart contract to make sure each pet had a real owner.

Excited, Milo found the cat he wanted and tapped the adoption button. The smart contract checked that he had enough digital coins, took his payment, and made him the new owner—all in just a few seconds!

"Wow, that was fast!" Milo said, watching his new cat blink on the screen.

But then his friend Zara gasped. "Milo! You forgot to pick a name! The smart contract already registered the adoption, and now you can't change it!"

Milo stared at his cat's official name—FluffernoodleSparkleToes III—which had been randomly chosen. His mouth dropped open. "Oh no! That wasn't the name I wanted!"

Zara burst out laughing. "That's the best name ever!"

Milo sighed, then chuckled. "Well, I guess smart contracts don't let you change your mind. Welcome to the family, FluffernoodleSparkleToes!"

1- What was Milo saving up to buy?

_____

2- How did the smart contract help with the adoption?

_____

3- Why couldn't Milo change the name of his pet?

_____

4- What lesson did Milo learn about smart contracts?

_____

5- Why did Zara think Milo's pet name was funny?

_____

THE SMART CONTRACT SURPRISE

In Bitville, people used smart contracts to make sure deals were fair. If you wanted to buy something, enter a contest, or even rent a bike, a smart contract handled everything automatically!

Milo had been saving up to buy a virtual pet—a Pixel Pals cat. The best part? The adoption process used a smart contract to make sure each pet had a real owner.

Excited, Milo found the cat he wanted and tapped the adoption button. The smart contract checked that he had enough digital coins, took his payment, and made him the new owner—all in just a few seconds!

"Wow, that was fast!" Milo said, watching his new cat blink on the screen.

But then his friend Zara gasped. "Milo! You forgot to pick a name! The smart contract already registered the adoption, and now you can't change it!"

Milo stared at his cat's official name—FluffernoodleSparkleToes III—which had been randomly chosen. His mouth dropped open. "Oh no! That wasn't the name I wanted!"

Zara burst out laughing. "That's the best name ever!"

Milo sighed, then chuckled. "Well, I guess smart contracts don't let you change your mind. Welcome to the family, FluffernoodleSparkleToes!"

What was Milo saving up to buy?
- **A virtual pet**

How did the smart contract help with the adoption?
- **It made sure the adoption was fair and fast**

Why couldn't Milo change the name of his pet?
- **The smart contract had already recorded it on the blockchain**

What lesson did Milo learn about smart contracts?
- **Once an agreement is made, it can't be changed**

Why did Zara think Milo's pet name was funny?
- **It was a super long and silly name**

Your Smart Contract, Your Rules!

Short Story/Essay Teachers Example Story

Sample

Title: My Smart Contract for Chores and Rewards

If I could create my own smart contract, I would design one to help kids earn rewards for completing chores. The smart contract would automatically track my finished chores and giving out rewards without needing my parents to check.

The contract would have a simple rule: If I finish my assigned chores, then I get a reward, like extra screen time or an allowance. If I don't complete my chores, then I don't get the reward. This would make sure everything is fair and no one can change the rules at the last minute. This smart contract is important because it helps families stay organized and not argue about if the chores were really done. Since smart contracts run on the blockchain, no one can change or erase the completed tasks, so the system is always fair. Parents wouldn't have to remember to hand out rewards, and kids would know exactly what they need to do to earn them.

Using a smart contract for chores would make life easier by keeping track of everything automatically. I would love to have a system like this at home!

Reflection Questions

At the end of the worksheet, students can answer a few reflection questions to wrap up their story.

Would you trust a smart contract to handle an important deal for you? Why or why not?

What would happen if someone tried to change the smart contract after it was created?

What new inventions or technology would make smart contracts even better?

YOUR SMART CONTRACT, YOUR RULES!

Name _____   Date _____

Create Your Own Smart Contract!

Imagine you get to design your own smart contract that follows simple "if-then" rules to make sure that agreements happen automatically.

Write a short essay about the smart contract you create!
Use your imagination!

1. What is your smart contract for?
   - Will it help people trade items, earn rewards, or keep track of tasks?
   - What problem does it solve?
2. How does your smart contract work?
   - What are the rules of your smart contract?
   - What happens if someone doesn't follow the rules?
3. Why is your smart contract important?
   - How does it make life easier, faster, or fairer?
   - Would you want to use it in real life? Why or why not?

_____

_____

_____

_____

_____

_____

_____

_____

_____

_____

_____

_____

_____

_____

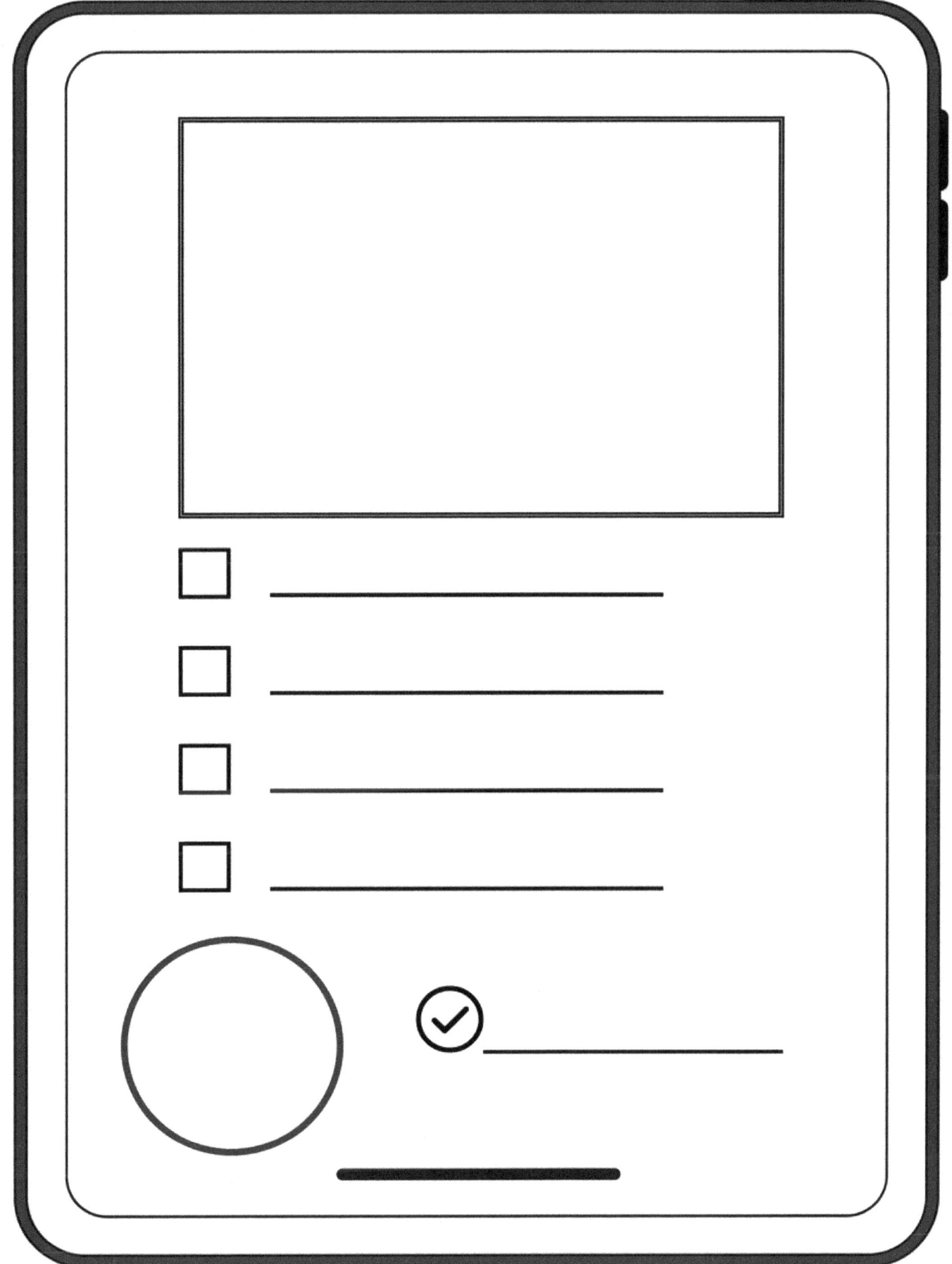

Decorate Your Birthday Cake:

🎂 If it's my birthday, I get _____ cupcakes!

🎉 Everyone must:
Wear _____ hats.
Say _____ (a silly word) when I arrive!

🚫 No one is allowed to say _____

🎁 Birthday Star Signature: _____

Design Your Friendship Bracelets!

💖 I, _____, and my
best friend _____, promise to:

Share our _____

🎉 Always _____

🚫 Never _____

💞 Signed with love:

❤️ _____
❤️ _____

📅 Design Your Weekly Chore Chart

🧹 I, _____, agree to do the following
chore: _____

📅 I will do this every: _____

🎁 If I do my chore, I get this reward:
_____

🙈 If I forget, I have to (do something funny):
_____

🖊 Signed: _____

🎨 Draw your pet here!

🐾 I, _____, promise to take care of
my pet named _____.

🐶 I will:
- Feed them every _____.
- Play with them for _____ minutes each day.

🐾 If I forget, I have to: _____

_____

_____.

🐾 Signed with a paw print: _____

Smart Contracts

Circle the correct answer for each question.

1.
- What is a smart contract?
- A) A digital agreement that runs automatically
- B) A contract that only lawyers can write
- C) A paper document that needs a signature
- D) A secret code that unlocks a computer

2.
- Which of these is something a smart contract can do?
- A) Give rewards automatically when conditions are met
- B) Wait for someone to approve every step
- C) Change its rules anytime someone wants
- D) Make people sign their name in person

3.
- Why are smart contracts useful?
- A) They make sure agreements happen exactly as written
- B) They let people change their minds anytime
- C) They slow down transactions for extra security
- D) They are only used by banks and lawyers

4.
- Where do smart contracts store information?
- A) On a chalkboard
- B) In a regular notebook
- C) On the blockchain
- D) Inside a video game

5.
- What happens when a smart contract's rules are met?
- A) The agreement runs automatically
- B) A person has to check it first
- C) It gets deleted
- D) It stops working until someone changes it

Quiz: Smart Contracts

Circle the correct answer for each question.

① • What is a smart contract?
  • **A)** A digital agreement that runs automatically
  • B) A contract that only lawyers can write
  • C) A paper document that needs a signature
  • D) A secret code that unlocks a computer

② • Which of these is something a smart contract can do?
  • **A)** Give rewards automatically when conditions are met
  • B) Wait for someone to approve every step
  • C) Change its rules anytime someone wants
  • D) Make people sign their name in person

③ • Why are smart contracts useful?
  • **A)** They make sure agreements happen exactly as written
  • B) They let people change their minds anytime
  • C) They slow down transactions for extra security
  • D) They are only used by banks and lawyers

④ • Where do smart contracts store information?
  • A) On a chalkboard
  • B) In a regular notebook
  • **C)** On the blockchain
  • D) Inside a video game

⑤ • What happens when a smart contract's rules are met?
  • **A)** The agreement runs automatically
  • B) A person has to check it first
  • C) It gets deleted
  • D) It stops working until someone changes it